Everyday Evangelising with Pope Francis

A HANDBOOK

by
Fr Donncha Ó hAodha

*All booklets are published thanks to the
generous support of the members of the
Catholic Truth Society*

CATHOLIC TRUTH SOCIETY

PUBLISHERS TO THE HOLY SEE

Contents

ISBN 978 1 78469 060 1

Everyday Evangelising

You and I are called to spread the Gospel in our everyday
lives. Each and all the faithful are naturally evangelisers
and they carry out this apostolate in the varied
circumstances of their ordinary lives. Every follower of
Christ has the capacity, privilege and duty of offering to
everyone by deed and word the Church's joyful message.
There is nothing more natural in the world for those who
have received the light of Christ than to radiate that light
for love of others.

The vocation of all the baptised to proclaim the joy of
the Gospel wherever they are, is one of the most constant
teachings of Pope Francis. This little "handbook" is not a
complete presentation of the Holy Father's teaching, but
is an attempt to show how the Pope is urging all of us to
rediscover our natural calling to spread the knowledge
and love of Christ and his Church in and through our
everyday lives.

The teaching of Pope Francis is encouraging and
challenging, and can help us renew our zeal to evangelise
as we consider the nature of our mission and the beauty of
our message. The Holy Father also offers helpful guidance
regarding how we can communicate Christ while facing
the challenges of evangelisation with determination,
serenity and faith in the power of the Holy Spirit.

The Mission

The best news ever

What is it that people most deeply desire? What do we all long for above anything else? Surely it is eternal happiness, full and unending life, perfect everlasting love. All of this, and to a degree beyond our most ambitious hopes, is contained in the Gospel. In fact, this fulness of life and love *is* the Gospel. God became man so that we might have life, and life to the full (cf. *Jn* 10:10). Christ himself is the Gospel and he is "the way, and the truth and the life" (*Jn* 14:6). Gospel precisely means "good news". In fact, it is the best news ever.

The loving Creator

The Gospel answers all our deepest queries and quandaries. The beauty of the world is no accident, nor are we meaningless beings stranded in the middle of a pointless universe. The world and the cosmos come from God who is Creator. He has no need to create anything outside himself, so the only reason for our existence is his pure, unadulterated, unconditional love. The Creator is not just all-powerful; he is also infinite love. Moreover God loves his creation; "he saw that it was very good" (*Gn* 1:25). The God of love is also the God of joy and peace. Indeed, as we make our pilgrim way in this life, with its inevitable ups and downs, the joy of the Lord is our strength (cf. *Ne* 8:10).

The merciful Redeemer

God is also our Saviour or Redeemer. Creation is wonderful and beautiful, but it is not perfect. While everything within nature tends towards life, death is ever present. Unforeseen natural disasters, uncontrollable personal tragedies, incurable illnesses all go to show that creation is "groaning in travail" (*Rm* 8:22). Human nature, while its basic goodness had not been destroyed, has nonetheless been wounded by sin (cf. *Gn* 3:16-19). Personal experience shows us that we have our weaknesses, that we are sinners, and that in fact at times we do wrong. Creation and every man and woman within it needs salvation. The human person, who is made for life, is subjected to physical death which came into the world through sin (cf. *Rm* 5:12).

The Creator did not abandon his creation however. If "the wage paid by sin is death…the present given by God is eternal life in Christ Jesus our Lord" (*Rm* 6:23). The Word through whom all things were made has become flesh and lived among us, full of grace and truth, (cf. *Jn* 1:3,14), and freely offers salvation to one and all. The overriding love of God is seen in the fact that his incarnate Son freely gave himself up for our sins in the Passion of his cross. The cross has become the tree of life, replacing the tree of death from which our first parents ate in the garden of Eden.

In Christ's incarnation, self-sacrificing death, and glorious Resurrection we have the ultimate answer to all our fears and questionings about the meaning of life and death. In Christ there is in fact a definitively positive answer to every fear and uncertainty, to every regret and guilt. Sickness, loneliness, failure and death are far from meaningless, but can be a true participation in the Passion of Jesus which gives way to the Resurrection. Jesus the Good Shepherd has come to save us from our sins by laying down his life for us (cf. *Jn* 10:11). He has come with infinite mercy to carry the stray sheep on his shoulders back to the fold of the eternal Father: "in him, we gain our freedom, the forgiveness of sins" (*Col* 1:17).

In fact the only true failure would be to knowingly and wilfully reject the saving love of God.

The Spirit of Love

After his Ascension to heaven, Christ did not leave us abandoned or orphaned (cf. *Jn* 14:18). Rather he sent the Holy Spirit, "the other Counsellor" (*Jn* 14:16) to be with us forever. The Spirit of Love lives continually in the family of the Church and in each of her members in grace.

Not only did God create us from pure love, and redeem us with infinite mercy, but he gives us the immense dignity of being his beloved children. "Think of the love that the Father has lavished on us, by letting us be called God's children; and that is what we are" (*1 Jn* 3:1). "What we *are*": we are not just called God's children; we are not just his children in a metaphorical way. In baptism we truly become beloved children of God in Christ by the working of the Holy Spirit. "Everyone moved by the Spirit is a son of God … it is the spirit of sons, and it makes us cry out, 'Abba, Father!' The Spirit himself and our spirit bear united witness that we are children of God" (*Rm* 8:14-16).

We are called not just to model our lives on Jesus Christ. The Christian life is not merely imitation of Christ; there is a real mystical *identification* with Christ. All the baptised can say with St Paul: "I live not now with my own life but but with the life of Christ who lives in me" (*Ga* 2:20).

Moreover as beloved children of God we are united as members of God's people, his family which is the Church, with bonds of mutual love and support which transcend all boundaries of space and time and are uninterrupted even by death. We "are no longer aliens or foreign visitors; you are citizens like all the saints, and part of God's household" (*Ep* 2:19).

The dignity of the Christian vocation is beyond humanity's most cherished hopes or expectations.

Intimacy with God

This ineffable intimacy with God is constantly strengthened and deepened in the sacraments which are true divine actions. Our union with the Lord reaches an unimagined depth through Holy Communion. By nourishing us with his flesh and blood, Jesus Christ makes us his "kith and kin" (cf. *Jn* 6:53-56). And throughout our lives the "gentle Father and God of all consolation" (*2 Co* 1:3) lovingly forgives, heals and strengthens us in the Sacrament of Penance and Reconciliation. God never refuses to forgive any sin for which we ask his pardon. The sacrament of divine mercy is the sacrament of true human liberation and the deepest joy.

The prophet Isaiah had announced that the Saviour would be called "Emmanuel", meaning "God is with us" (cf. *Is* 7:14, *Mt* 1:23). The amazing closeness of God to us is seen in creation, redemption, and in the process of our sanctification. God is not just near us; he is "with us". He dwells within those who live in his grace. As Jesus promised at the Last Supper: "If anyone loves me he will keep my word, and my Father will love him, and we shall come to him and make our home with him" (*Jn* 14:23).

Truly, the only danger is to underestimate the beauty and joy of the Gospel.

The Call

All are called to holiness

The Blessed Trinity's closeness to us means that our whole life is "charged with the grandeur of God", to use the poetic expression of Gerard Manley Hopkins. By the grace of baptism we are called and enabled to seek holiness and to spread holiness, to collaborate with the Holy Spirit in sanctifying ourselves and the world around us. The all-embracing love of God invites every single member of the faithful to the fulness of charity which is Christian sanctity. The Lord summarises much of his teaching in the Sermon on the Mount, in the phrase: "You must therefore be perfect just as your heavenly Father is perfect" (*Mt* 5:48).

As beloved children of God, nothing in our lives is indifferent or unimportant to God. Every hair on our head is counted (*Lk* 12:7). Our most apparently insignificant deeds can be acts of faith, hope and love. Through the grace of the Holy Spirit, our daily work and family life can become a living prayer of thanksgiving, praise, love and reparation. The life of each and every Christian can be a great act of adoration. And at the end of our earthly life the Lord eagerly awaits us in heaven, in the company of Our Lady, the angels and the saints, that great "cloud of witnesses" (*Heb* 12:1) who lovingly surrounded and supported us during our earthly life.

This divine adventure of creation, redemption and sanctification, in which we are all invited to take part, is the Gospel proclaimed by the Church. Good news spreads and the best news spreads most powerfully. Catholics are not just passive recipients of the treasures of God's love but active transmitters of that Gospel which in his infinite mercy the Lord offers to each and every man and woman. The light of grace, the fire of God's life in us, cannot be hidden or subdued. Rather Christ entrusts us with a demanding and enthralling mission: "your light must shine in the sight of men, so that, seeing your good works, they may give the praise to your Father in heaven" (*Mt* 5:16).

All are called to spread the Gospel

Each and all the baptised, whatever our personal circumstances, are called to spread the joy of the Gospel in our daily lives. This is one of Pope Francis's constant teachings and is central to his 2013 Apostolic Exhortation on "The Joy of the Gospel", *Evangelii Gaudium* (*EG*).

The Holy Father does not limit himself to reminding us of the fact that the call to evangelise is an essential part of the Christian vocation. He also offers many helpful explanations of why this is the case, and teases out how we might live out our apostolic mission in ordinary everyday life.

For our part, we may have questions or doubts about the vocation to be apostles. Why is seeking to spread the Faith essential to being a follower of Christ? Might this not be a task only for experts, for priests, or for members of the Church who have received a special consecration or missionary calling? Is proposing the Catholic faith compatible with respect for other religions?

Perhaps we may hesitate before a task which seems overwhelming. We may fear that it is beyond our capacities, or that our sins and inadequacies make us unfit to proclaim Christ.

Our concerns may also be of a practical nature. How can I spread the Gospel in my family and workplace on a daily basis? What does this mean in practice? How can I face challenges such as indifference, secularism, disaffection from the Church?

Perhaps we are already trying to live out our vocation to evangelise. How can we overcome weariness or keep faith when the results seem slow or non-existent? What are the fundamental motives for evangelising? How does the effort to go out to others help each of us in turn? Who can we look on as models and intercessors in our daily apostolate?

Our Lord charged St Peter with confirming his brothers and sisters in the Faith (cf. *Lk* 22:32). Pope Francis is doing just this in reminding us of our apostolic capacity and responsibility. He is encouraging us to persevere in this beautiful and demanding task, which is for the glory of God and the benefit of all mankind, starting with ourselves. The evangeliser is the first one to benefit from evangelising.

To be a Christian is to be an apostle

Central to the Holy Father's teaching is the fact that each and every one of the faithful are called to proclaim Christ, because by their very identity Christians are naturally evangelisers. Why is this so?

The apostolic mission of the Church is none other than the continuation through time of the divine mission whereby God is inviting all to salvation. The Gospel is the account of God's merciful love affair with mankind and with the whole of creation. After the entrance of sin into history (cf. *Gn* 2:14-19), God *sent* his only-begotten Son into the world to redeem it, to save it. After Christ's Ascension, the Father and the Son *sent* the Holy Spirit to perpetuate Christ's saving *mission* in the Church until the end of the world (the Latin for "sending" is *missio*).

The mission of the Church and of each of her members is the prolongation in history of this conjoined mission of the Son and the Spirit. Jesus tells us in the Gospel: "As the Father sent me, so am I sending you" (*Jn* 20:21) Hence it is not just that the Church *has* a mission; she *is* a mission. In a word, the Church and each of her members are essentially missionary.

We become part of and take on the saving mission of the Son and the Holy Spirit through baptism. As Pope Francis teaches, "all the baptised, whatever their position in the Church…are agents of evangelisation" (*EG* 120). Thus all the faithful can truly be Spirit-filled evangelisers. Through the sacraments, Christians "put on Christ" (*Ga* 3:27) and by living in grace they truly "are" his active presence in the world.

A light to others

To be immersed in Christ and to announce him are inseparable aspects of the reality of being Catholic. To be identified with the Saviour is to share in his zeal "to preach good news to the poor" (*Lk* 4:18). To be bathed in the One who is the "light of the world" (*Jn* 8:12), is to become living beacons which convey his saving radiance (cf. *Mt* 5:15).

St John Chrysostom (who died in 407), one of the greatest preachers in the history of the Church, put it like this: "It easier for the sun not to give heat, not to shine, than for the Christian not to send forth light; it is easier for the light to be darkness than for this to be so…

It is not possible for the light of a Christian to be hid; it is not possible for a lamp so conspicuous as that to be concealed."[1]

The evangelising mission of the Church is lived out in a myriad of unassuming ways: parents who teach their children to work well and direct their efforts to God; the sick and the lonely who offer their sufferings in union with Christ's Passion; workers, professionals and business people, farmers, educators and politicians whose ethical attitude and actions constitute a living catechesis; those who dedicate themselves to the less well off, those who in different ways promote the Gospel of life; the faithful who pray for the Church and the world.

Christ works through us

The effort then to spread the Gospel is not an optional extra or an "add-on" activity for some supposedly "more committed" Catholics. It is an essential part of every Christian's identity. To live in Christ, to be identified with him (cf. *Ga* 2:20), is to share in his desire and work for the salvation of all souls. "In union with Jesus," says Pope Francis, "we seek what he seeks and we love what he loves" (*EG* 267).

---

[1] St John Chrysostom, *Homily 20, 4 on the Acts of the Apostles.*

Christ wills to work in and through us, notwithstanding our inadequacies and defects. The evangelising vocation of each and every one of the baptised is beautifully expressed in the prayer of St Teresa of Avila:

> Christ has no body now but yours,
> No hands, no feet on earth but yours,
> Yours are the eyes with which he looks with
>   compassion on this world,
> Yours are the feet with which he walks to do good,
> Yours are the hands with which he blesses all
>   the world.

A Universal Task

Always and everywhere and to everyone

Given the variety of vocations and situations of those who make up the People of God, the ways in which Christ is proclaimed are innumerable. What is essential to the life of the Church and to each of her members is to share in Christ's zeal to spread his fire of love. This will happen in all sorts of ways since, as the Holy Father points out, "being a disciple means being constantly ready to bring the love of Jesus to others, and this can happen unexpectedly and in any place: on the street, in a city square, during work, on a journey" (*EG* 127).

The mission we are engaged in is truly "catholic", that is to say "universal". It is for *all* the faithful to bring *all* Christ's message to *all* people, times and places. Before his Ascension, Jesus entrusted his followers with a universal mandate. Our Lord invoked "*all* authority on heaven and on earth" and charged *all* his followers of *all* places and *all* times to proclaim *all* of the Gospel to *all* nations, teaching them to observe *all* that he had commanded (cf. *Mt* 28:19-20). Lest we be overwhelmed by this mission, Christ pledged he would be with his Church at *all* times. On this basis, Pope Francis urges us to "go forth to offer everyone the life of Jesus Christ" (*EG* 49).

This "going forth" takes on innumerable forms depending on the different situations in which Christians find themselves. Most "apostolate" or "evangelisation" is never recognised or called as such and yet is an authentic proclamation of Christ. The smile of a tired parent, a job well done for the love of God, refinement in dealing with a customer or an employee, an expression of sympathy or forgiveness, hidden pain offered up, an uncharitable conversation tactfully redirected, a prudent change of television channels, fidelity to one's spouse, teaching the content of the Faith to family and friends, efforts to improve society with particular care for the poor: all constitute an affirmation of the joy of Christ's presence.

Proclaiming Christ naturally, in conversations and through friendships

The history of the Church can rightly be seen as a history of conversations and friendships. Andrew followed Jesus first and then he introduced his brother Simon to the Lord (cf. *Jn* 1:40-42). Christ called Philip, who in turn sought out Nathanael and challenged him to "come and see" for himself (cf. *Jn* 1:43-46). Indeed "faith comes from what is preached" (*Rm* 10:17) and the words which invite us to follow Christ are very often those of parents or relatives, friends, neighbours or colleagues.

As the Gospel shows, often the most natural and effective Christian witness is that of one's peers. At World Youth Day in Brazil in 2013, Pope Francis challenged the over three million young people present - and by extension the entire Church - to embrace the Lord's command to go and announce the Gospel. In this context the Holy Father preached: "Do you know what is the best tool for evangelising the young? Another young person. That is the path for all of you to follow" (Homily, 28th July 2013).

The Church has always grown in this spontaneous organic way. As St John Paul II wrote, "God uses human friendship to lead hearts to the sources of divine charity".[2] Indeed, what could be more natural than for people who appreciate and love one another to share what they value most? Friends and family help one another in countless ways, such as passing on helpful experience or advice about work or sports or health. Why should it be any different when it comes to sharing the greatest and most lasting goods?

The example of your faith

St Josemaría Escrivá was called by God to remind everyone of the universal call to holiness. The founder of Opus Dei spent his whole life explaining how each and

---

[2] John Paul II, *Message for World Youth Day 2004*, 7.

every member of the Church is called to the fulness of sanctity and apostolate in virtue of his or her baptism. Accordingly he stressed how lay people become saints and spread the Gospel in and through their daily life and ordinary work.

In one of his homilies he explains how true friendship spontaneously becomes apostolate:

> The Christian apostolate - and I'm talking about an ordinary Christian living as just one more man or woman among equals - is a great work of teaching. Through real, personal, loyal friendship, you create in others a hunger for God and you help them to discover new horizons - naturally, simply. With the example of your faith lived to the full, with a loving word which is full of the force of divine truth. Be daring. Count on the help of Mary, queen of apostles (*Christ is Passing By*, n. 149).

Apostolate is loving service

To seek to spread the Gospel is to freely offer the gift of a treasure which has been freely received. Christian apostles seek to develop the qualities most conducive to this mission: approachability, readiness for dialogue, patience, warmth, as well as the art of listening. St Paul speaks of becoming all things to all men for the sake of their salvation (cf. *1 Co* 9:22). In fully assuming our innate vocation to evangelise, we will often be challenged to hone our personality as we try to develop virtues and qualities which will make us better transmitters of God's message.

Pope Francis's teaching on the need to clearly proclaim Christ to all, while at the same time respecting the freedom of all, echoes that of his predecessor. Benedict XVI also offered clear teaching on these two inseparable demands of apostolic charity:

> We impose nothing, yet we propose ceaselessly, as Peter recommends in one of his Letters: "In your hearts, reverence Christ as Lord. Always be prepared to make a defence to anyone who calls you to account for the hope that is in you" (*1 P* 3:15). And everyone, in the end, asks this of us, even those who seem not to. From personal and communal experience, we know well that it is Jesus whom everyone awaits (Homily, 14th May 2010).

Practical help

Today as in the past, many people come to Christ through the example and words of relatives and friends. Individuals discover or rediscover the sacraments through the example and words of a colleague or neighbour. Others come to discern their vocation in life thanks to the encouragement they received to read the Gospels, the *Catechism of the Catholic Church* or some helpful book or website. Other souls are shown that there is hope and that life is worth living, through the upright lifestyle or charitable deeds of a friend or acquaintance.

The "peripheries" Pope Francis is urging us to embrace may often be reached by means of a conversation across the kitchen table or over a pint of beer in a pub. The Gospel is to be shared naturally and affectionately in the most diverse and normal settings; in the hospital ward, on the factory floor, on the way home from school, in the university department, at the taxi rank or in the gym.

The evangeliser is the first to benefit

Pope Francis has often evoked a phrase of Blessed Paul VI: "the comforting joy of evangelising" (*EG* 10). It is important to keep this joy in mind, especially when proclaiming Christ is more challenging. The call to spread the Gospel is not a burden. It is a gift of God to his beloved children.

St Thérèse of Lisieux, the young Carmelite affectionately known as the "Little Flower", was keenly aware of her vocation to apostolate, especially through prayer. Indeed it is significant that the Patroness of the Missions is a young nun who never left the few square metres of her cloister. With her holiness she reached the whole world.

In one of her letters to her sister Céline (written on 15th August 1892), she raises a question which could well occur to any of us: why does the Lord involve Christians in the work of evangelisation when he is all-powerful and has no need of our collaboration? She wrote:

> How mysterious it is! Is not Jesus all-powerful? Do not creatures belong to him who made them? Why then does Jesus say: "Pray the Lord of the harvest to send labourers"? Why? Surely because Jesus has so incomprehensible a love for us, that he wants us to have a share with him in the salvation of souls. He wants to do nothing without us. The creator of the universe waits for the prayer of a poor little soul to save other souls redeemed like it at the price of all his Blood.

Without any merit on our part, the Lord invites each and all, notwithstanding our failures and shortcomings, to be channels of divine love. This reality is not just a responsibility for each of the faithful, much less a weight, but a gift and an opportunity. To seek to evangelise matures us humanly and spiritually, and leads to the fulfilment of the Christian vocation. As St John Vianney put it in one of his catechetical instructions: "To pray and to love, that is the happiness of man on earth". Evangelisation is to pray and to love. We are the first to benefit from our intrinsic vocation as "fishers of men" (*Mt* 4:19).

The Message

The saving Word

What is the message to be transmitted? What is the Gospel to be spread? Pope Francis reminds us that the proclamation is not so much a "what" as a *"who"*: Jesus Christ. "The heart of [the] message will always be the same: the God who revealed his immense love in the crucified and risen Christ" (*EG* 11).

The *Letter to the Hebrews* begins by affirming that "at various times in the past and in various different ways, God spoke to our ancestors through the prophets; but in our own time, the last days, he has spoken to us through his Son" (1:1-2). God gradually revealed himself through the words of the great book of Creation by natural revelation, then also by supernatural revelation through the inspired words of the history of the Old Covenant, of the patriarchs and prophets and in the sacred songs of Israel.

But when the time had fully come, "the Word was made flesh [and] lived among us" (*Jn* 1:14). Jesus Christ is, as the Second Vatican Council teaches, "both the mediator and the fulness of all revelation" (*Dei Verbum* 2). This same "Word of life", Jesus Christ, continues to live and act in his Church; the baptised live in, with and from him, and invite all mankind to the fulness of joy in communion with him (cf. *1 Jn* 1:1-4).

Invitation to share friendship

The message is not just information; the message is a living Person: Christ. Loving communion with Jesus and communicating Jesus to others are inseparably at the heart of every healthy Christian life. Enjoying Christ's friendship naturally involves inviting others to share in this friendship. To live the Gospel is to spread the Gospel. To be united to the Word incarnate is to proclaim the Word incarnate. This reality is simply yet powerfully expressed in St Patrick's Breastplate:

> Christ with me,
> Christ before me,
> Christ behind me,
> Christ within me,
> Christ below me,
> Christ above me,
> Christ on my right hand,
> Christ on my left hand,
> Christ in my lying,
> Christ in my sitting,
> Christ in my standing,
> Christ in the heart of everyone who thinks of me,

Christ in the mouth of everyone who speaks to me,
Christ in every eye which looks upon me,
Christ in every ear which listens to me.

What we seek to transmit is knowledge and love of the Person of Christ, our merciful Saviour, who leads us to the Father, by the Holy Spirit. We seek to communicate Christ in every way possible: by prayer and sacrifice, by example and words, and by the attractiveness of genuine charity within the Church.

To evangelise also means transmitting knowledge of sacred Scripture and of the Church's creed. We seek to share "the infinite treasure of Christ" (*Ep* 3:8), and so our message is always a fresh, positive and beautiful proposition. Hence while the Lord's moral teaching is demanding it is profoundly human and satisfying. In this regard Pope Francis encourages us to be "joyful messengers of challenging proposals" (*EG* 168). Here again there is a clear continuity of emphasis with the moral teaching of Benedict XVI who repeatedly emphasised that the Commandments are not a series of negative prohibitions but rather a great "yes" to God, to creation, to human dignity and to true life.

Helping others to get to know Christ personally

The evangelisation of each individual is different because each soul is unique. One person may be inspired by the example of a friend, another by a good book, another by the faith experienced in the family, or by the beauty of the liturgy. In every case, to welcome the Gospel is to embrace the Lord Jesus, to respond freely to the love of God given to us in Christ (cf. 1 *Jn* 4:9), to enter into a personal relationship with the Lord.

Pope Francis tells us:

> I never tire of repeating those words of Benedict XVI which take us to the very heart of the Gospel: "Being a Christian is not the result of an ethical choice or a lofty idea, but the encounter with an event, a person, which gives life a new horizon and a decisive direction"(*EG* 7).

In this context we can understand the Holy Father's consistent emphasis from the start of his pontificate on the Sacrament of Reconciliation, since we all need the mercy of God, and because the forgiveness of our sins is always the door to greater intimacy with Christ.

This idea is like an encouraging refrain throughout Pope Francis's preaching: God never tires of forgiving us; we are the ones who tire of seeking his mercy. Often a good confession is a moment of unprecedented evangelisation where the Lord draws us to himself very deeply and effectively. Through the practice of frequent confession many families are built up, vocations are discerned and the zeal to spread the Gospel grows.

To evangelise, then, is also to speak about God's mercy and do all we can to promote the Sacrament of Penance, following the example of the Holy Father. Indeed before his Ascension the Lord opened the minds of his apostles to understand the Scriptures and told them "that, in his name, repentance for the forgiveness of sins would be preached to all the nations" (*Lk* 24:47).

Shine through me

Because the Gospel is God's saving love in Christ, it is inherently beautiful and a message of true joy. The challenge in our daily apostolate is, notwithstanding our limitations, to spread around us "the incense of Christ" (cf. *2 Co* 2:15). This is the sentiment expressed in a beautiful prayer of Blessed John Henry Newman:

> Dear Jesus,
> Help me to spread thy fragrance everywhere I go.
> Flood my soul with thy spirit and life.
> Penetrate and possess my whole being so utterly
> that all my life may only be a radiance of thine.
> Shine through me,
> and be so in me that every soul that I come
> in contact with
> may feel thy presence in my soul.
> Let them look up and see no longer me
> but only Jesus![3]

---

[3] From Newman's meditation "Jesus the Light of the Soul", also known as "Radiating Christ" or "The Fragrance Prayer".

Ways and Means

How to go about it

Thus far all may seem clear enough: we are all called to evangelise, and this daily apostolate is about communicating Christ and the teaching of his Church. But how does one go about this in practice? What are the means to offer the Catholic faith to everyone around us?

And perhaps even more to the point, how can we face the obvious challenges? What can we do when we encounter difficulties or when we seem to be rowing against the tide, or hitting a wall of indifference, or battling what seems like an overwhelming force in the opposite direction in the culture or society around us?

Pope Francis constantly reminds us of the fundamental truth of all apostolate, namely that it is first and foremost and fundamentally the Lord's work. Evangelisation is, as we have seen, the continuation through history of the saving and sanctifying missions of the Son and the Holy Spirit. As such it is a divine work and so if we feel that it is beyond our capacities, we are quite right; we spread the Gospel only insofar as God works through us.

Put out into the deep

It is helpful to contemplate the apostles on the lake of Gennesaret, exhausted and disappointed after having toiled all night and caught nothing. It is precisely then that the Lord urges them to "put out into the deep" and let down their nets for a catch (*Lk* 5:4). The humility and faith of St Peter and the others is admirable. Going against their better judgement and after a futile night of hard work, they obey Christ's instruction. They had faith in the Master, and this faith was richly rewarded: "They netted such a huge number of fish that their nets began to tear, so they signalled to their companions in the other boat to come and help them" (*Lk* 5:6-7).

We can all identify with St Peter's awareness of his own inadequacy to be an evangeliser. After the miraculous catch of fish he "fell at the knees of Jesus saying, 'Leave me, Lord; I am a sinful man'" (*Lk* 5:8). He who was to become the Prince of the Apostles expresses his conviction that the task is well beyond him. What is most significant in this conversation is how the Lord replies to Peter: "Do not be afraid; from now on it is men you will catch" (*Lk* 5:10).

What is decisive, what makes all the difference, what renders Peter an effective apostle is his union with Christ and with Christ's mission. As Benedict XVI once put it, "in order to become fishers of men with Christ one first needs to be 'caught' by him" (Homily, 14th June 2008). The same goes for all of us. Our apostolate will be fruitful to the extent that we are united to Christ.

Prayer comes first

At the Last Supper Jesus explained: "I am the vine, you are the branches. Whoever remains in me, with me in him, bears fruit in plenty; for cut off from me you can do nothing" (*Jn* 15:5). What is absolutely crucial is to seek to be united to Christ. No one can give what he does not have. To draw others into friendship with Christ, we must be the Lord's friend in the first place.

Communion with Christ leads to communion with our brothers and sisters, since to be one with Christ is to be one with his people. Evangelisation builds unity with God and among ourselves. In fact the Second Vatican Council describes the Church precisely in these terms: "The Church, in Christ, is in the nature of sacrament - a sign and instrument, that is, of communion with God and of unity among all men" (*Lumen Gentium* 1). In other words, evangelisation is the building up of the mystical Body, of the People of God, of God's family, of the Church.

Apostolate, the desire to spread the Good News, is a question of living out the great double commandment of love of God and neighbour. Indeed, "mission is at once a passion for Jesus and a passion for his people" (*EG* 268). Just as we reach out to those who are materially in need, we also seek to alleviate those who are spiritually hungry and at times even spiritually destitute.

Ongoing formation

To reach further in apostolate we must deepen in prayer through participation in the sacraments, by offering sacrifices and meditating on the Word of God. In trying to speak openly about Christ and his Church our own faith is deepened, and we learn over time how best to articulate it. Because we want to witness to others, we will be motivated to take greater care of our own ongoing formation. We will be led to study Scripture and Catholic doctrine more deeply and reflect on how best to communicate it.

To persevere in proclaiming Christ is not a question of emotional enthusiasm, but rather the natural result of union with God. Our life "with Christ in God" (*Col* 3:3) spills over to help and benefit others, just as we in turn are often carried along by the prayer life and holiness of others.

Prayer, communication and communion with the Lord, is the necessary basis and prerequisite of all evangelisation. That is why the Holy Father stresses:

…without prolonged moments of adoration, of prayer-ful encounter with the word, of sincere conversation with the Lord, our work easily becomes meaningless; we lose energy as a result of weariness and difficulties, and our fervour dies out. The Church urgently needs the deep breath of prayer, and to my great joy groups devoted to prayer and intercession, the prayerful reading of God's word and the perpetual adoration of the Eucharist are growing at every level of ecclesial life (*EG* 262).

There is a wonderful paradox at work here. When we feel a greater responsibility for others, when we seek to save souls with Christ, the first step we take is to deepen our own spiritual life. We ourselves become the first beneficiaries of our efforts to do apostolate with others. Evangelisation stretches us in a very healthy way in human terms and in spiritual terms. Moreover the daily self-giving that the Christian apostolate implies leads us to imitate and take part in the self-giving of Christ (cf. *Ph* 2:4-7). Living more for others increases our identification with Jesus.

Relying on the grace of God

The Pope's emphasis on the spiritual life as the primary source of evangelisation is ever timely and relevant. It is all too human for us to put our trust in what *we* do or say, and we can easily forget that all apostolic fruitfulness comes from the grace of God. There is always a danger of "activism", of thinking that what makes apostolate fruitful is primarily our efforts, or given programmes or structures for evangelisation.

Of course we must do all we can by deed and word to proclaim Christ. And of course there is always a need for projects or methods to facilitate the Church's apostolate. The challenge is to do all we can without ever losing sight of the fact that without Christ we can do nothing (cf. *Jn* 15:5), and conversely that we can do all things in him who strengthens us (cf. *Ph* 4:13).

An effective antidote to self-reliance is prayer of intercession, which the Holy Father recommends in a particular way. Praying for others is crucial for evangelisation since it is the first and most powerful means we have to reach souls. At the same time, interceding for others greatly enriches our own spiritual life. By entrusting others to the Lord, be they loved ones or strangers, passers-by on the street, fellow-passengers on the train or people on the television screen, the faithful deepen their contemplative spirit in ordinary everyday life.

Witnessing first by deeds

Jesus Christ set out "to do and teach" (cf. *Ac* 1:1). We too proclaim the Gospel first of all by our deeds. The Second Vatican Council states that God has revealed himself "by deeds and words, which are intrinsically bound up with each other" (*DV* 2). This same dynamic obtains in the work of evangelisation. Actions speak louder than words. Moreover, apostolic deeds open the way to conversation about Christ.

Experience shows time and again how souls are drawn to the Church by the example of ordinary Christians' fidelity to Christ. Sometimes people are inspired by the example of serenity and patience in suffering. On other occasions the example of a Catholic who does his or her work as well as possible with a spirit of service and concern for the less well off is a powerful stimulus.

Evangelisation can sometimes be a seemingly chance encounter. A stranger who goes out of his or her way to help in an emergency, a helpful conversation on the bus, the fidelity of spouses and their openness to new life: all of these deeds of love are eloquent witness to Jesus Christ.

The faith of Catholics will naturally be expressed in their external activities, since faith is not just expressed in words, but above all in deeds. In light of the vocation to everlasting life, the apostle always seeks to improve him or herself, to be a steward to and beautify creation, to enjoy and develop culture, build up society, solve problems and help others. In other words, evangelisation always has a positive social dimension. As the history of the Church shows, Christianity is profoundly humanising. To seek to improve at our work, to be a better parent, worker, scientist, artist, gardener, cook, homemaker, teacher or nurse, is not only compatible with being a good Catholic, but is a natural part of seeking to be an apostle in the midst of the world.

Speaking about God

Referring to missionary work, St Paul declares: "They will not believe in him unless they have heard of him, and they will not hear of him unless they get a preacher" (*Rm* 10:14). The Christian mission always involves speaking about Christ, who is the saving Word. Implicit proclamation by example alone is not enough. "There can be no true evangelisation without the explicit proclamation of Jesus as Lord" says Pope Francis (*EG* 110).

Sometimes we may be unsure how to bring up the topic or what is the best way to express the Faith to others. Of course it will depend on the given context, but usually it will be the very natural apostolate of conversations with family, friends and acquaintances. Most often our words will simply be an expression of our own experience of Christ, the sacraments and prayer, of how the Gospel challenges us to improve and helps us in our daily life. In other words we'll try to give an account of the hope that is in us (cf. *1 Pt* 3:15).

On reflection we may realise that those who most helped us towards Christ were not exceptionally erudite or articulate. They sought to be instruments of the Word, and what they had to say was given to them, as Christ promised. It was not they who were speaking but the Spirit of the Father speaking through them (cf. *Mt* 10:19-20).

Love, joy and beauty

It is well known that in the early Church many people came to believe through the unity and charity they witnessed among the first Christians. Love continues to be the most powerful proclamation of the triune God who "is love" (*1 Jn* 4:8). Tertullian records that pagans of his day were drawn by the fraternal charity of believers. "See how they love one another", they said.

Communion within the Church testifies to the truth of her message. Hence it is clear how ecumenism and evangelisation are closely connected. The Holy Father points out also that unity and fraternity are not just challenges on the global or institutional level. The "new Commandment" (*Jn* 13:34) is always *new* since we can always grow in love and we will always have to fight the danger of division, especially within the "household of faith" (cf. *Ga* 6:10).

As with any large and diverse family, within the Church, there will naturally be a variety of styles and differences in matters of opinion. The daily effort to grow in love by understanding and forgiving, within the family, company, school, parish or sports club is a genuine proclamation of the Gospel. On a practical note the Holy Father points out that "to pray for a person with whom I am irritated is a beautiful step forward in love, and an act of evangelisation. Let us do it today!" (*EG* 101).

Love and joy are inseparable as fruits of the Holy Spirit (cf. *Ga* 5:22). This is why the proclamation of Christ, in whom we know what love is (cf. *1 Jn* 4:9-10) is an intrinsically joyous reality. Cheerfulness in the ups and downs of daily life and the joy of faith even in the midst of great suffering can be a powerful reflection of Christ.

Caring for others, starting with prayer and penance; deeds of charity and disinterested service; the effort to sanctify our daily work and make the world a better place; fraternity and forgiveness within families and other communities, and especially communion within the Church; the proclamation of Christ in our own words and with joy, even when we are under pressure or suffering: all these aspects of the typical apostolate of ordinary Catholics are expressions of what Pope Francis calls the "way of beauty", along which many people can discover the truth of the Gospel.

Dealing with Difficulties

While surveying the ways and means of apostolate, there may be a nagging doubt in the back of our minds: "But it is not plain sailing!" "It is not so easy in practice." Indeed, on a certain level, it is not.

Salvation is a fruit of the cross. As Christ carried out our redemption through his Passion, so too, to appropriate and spread the offer of eternal life involves suffering with Jesus. To offer efforts and sacrifices for others is essential to evangelisation. Thus the great apostle Paul rejoiced in his sufferings as in his flesh he made up "all that still has to be undergone by Christ for the sake of his body, the Church" (*Col* 1:24). Those who share more closely in the cross, for example the sick or incapacitated, have in fact a particularly valuable contribution to make to the spread of the Gospel. The great Christian paradox, "it is when I am weak that I am strong" (*2 Co* 12:10), is a living reality in the Church's apostolate.

When Christ died on the cross the veil of the temple was ripped from top to bottom (cf. *Mt* 27:51). There was no longer any separation between God and his people. Christ had made "peace by his death on the cross" (*Col* 1:20). The gulf caused by sin was bridged by the Lord's self-giving suffering.

The difficulties the Church and each of the faithful come across in the task of evangelisation are a sharing in that saving cross which breaks down barriers between human beings and God. In one of his homilies, referring to the sufferings of the early Church, Pope Francis observed: "At the very moment when persecution broke out, the Church's missionary nature also 'broke out'" (Homily, 23rd April 2013). The challenges in evangelisation are part of evangelisation.

Certainly there are difficulties, these are to be expected, and by the grace of God obstacles and sufferings can become effective means of apostolate. For "we all have to experience many hardships…before we enter the kingdom of God" (*Ac* 14:22). If the temptation to discouragement looms, we can remember the encouraging words of Pope Francis:

> Challenges exist to be overcome! Let us be realists, but without losing our joy, our boldness and our hope-filled commitment. Let us not allow ourselves to be robbed of missionary vigour! (*EG* 109)

Challenges within ourselves

Broadly speaking, there are two kinds of challenges in the mission: from within ourselves and from outside ourselves. Starting with the former, we may recognise some of our own temptations and weaknesses in Pope Francis's incisive words about the temptation "to be that kind of Christian who keeps the Lord's wounds at arm's length" (*EG* 270). For different reasons we may fail to go out of ourselves and commit ourselves to apostolate. Our own limitations, failings and sins are often the greatest challenge to launching out in evangelisation.

It is instructive to reflect that at the moment of the Ascension, when "the eleven disciples set out for Galilee, to the mountain where Jesus had arranged to meet them. When they saw him, they fell down before him; though some hesitated" (*Mt* 28:16-17). *Though some hesitated?* We might wonder at this. How was it possible for them to doubt Jesus having lived so closely with him, heard his sublime words and witnessed numerous miracles, especially his Resurrection? How could they doubt after the risen Lord had "shown himself alive to them after his Passion by many demonstrations; for forty days he had continued to appear to them and tell them about the kingdom of God" (*Ac* 1:3)?

They doubted because they were human like we are. And as we know, this weakness on the part of his apostles did not deter the Lord from conferring on them the universal apostolic mission: "Go therefore, make disciples of all the nations…" (*Mt* 28:19). What matters is the call of the Master to evangelise, and our effort to respond to that invitation.

Sometimes the difficulty is that we are afraid to proclaim Christ. Apostolate requires daring, especially where the Christian message is counter-cultural or politically incorrect. Even in traditionally Catholic environments it may not be usual for individual Christians to speak openly among themselves about their faith.

In any event this is not a new challenge. Witnessing to Christ has always required fortitude. The example of the apostles Peter and John may come to mind. Having been forbidden to speak any more about Christ, they simply and boldly reply "We cannot stop proclaiming what we have seen and heard" (*Ac* 4:20).

It takes heroic courage to witness to Christ by one's blood as is the case of so many Christians in our own times. We know it can also take an effort to step out of our comfort zone to broach a more personal topic with a friend or family member, or to suggest to a colleague or neighbour the possibility of considering prayer, returning to the sacraments, or helping out with some apostolic venture.

We are not on our own however. Rather, we are sharing in the mission of the Holy Spirit who is the soul of the Church. The strength to spread the Faith comes from God. By the same token, the effectiveness of evangelisation, whether we perceive it or not, is totally disproportionate to our efforts. Thus, in order to grow in the *parrhesia* or apostolic boldness which Pope Francis often speaks about, we would do well to ask the Paraclete to help us be humble and effective instruments of his love. Before a more challenging conversation, or if we have to give clear public witness to the Church's teaching, or whenever we are conscious of our own inadequacy, we can invoke the Holy Spirit to work through our weakness.

We may also need to battle with our own sluggishness. "Why bother?"; "It's too hard"; "I cannot do it". Pope Francis is asking us to shake off this inertia. We have already seen the Holy Father's teaching on how we are the first to benefit humanly and spiritually from the effort to spread the Gospel. We evangelise in order to be evangelised. We grow in holiness in so far as we give ourselves to others.

The Pope also faces us squarely with our responsibility for one another:

> If something should rightly disturb us and trouble our consciences, it is the fact that so many of our brothers and sisters are living without the strength, light and consolation born of friendship with Jesus Christ, without a community of faith to support them, without meaning and a goal in life. (EG 49)

Above all we seek to spread the Gospel for a very natural reason since goodness always tends to spread. It makes perfect sense to seek to share with others what we are convinced to be the ultimate good news, the source of everlasting fulfilment and joy. As Pope St Gregory the Great put it in one of his homilies:

When you discover that something has been of benefit to you, you want to tell others about it. In the same way, you should want others to accompany you along the ways of the Lord. If you are going to the forum or the baths and you run into someone with time on his hands, you invite him to go with you. Apply this human behaviour to the spiritual realm and when you go towards God, do not go alone.[4]

External difficulties

A second set of challenges are the obstacles external to us. There are indeed real difficulties but the grace of God is also real, and is always more powerful. Nonetheless, it sometimes seems that our efforts are futile because they meet a great wall of indifference. This can be the case especially in more affluent and secularised environments. This challenge is also an opportunity to grow in faith through perseverance.

The strength to keep evangelising is not based on apparent success but on loyalty to every human person who can rightly say to God, along with St Augustine: "You have made us for yourself, and our hearts are restless until they can find rest in you".[5]

---

[4] St Gregory the Great, *Homiliae in Evangelia*, 6,6.
[5] St Augustine, *Confessions* 1,1,1; cf. *Catechism of the Catholic Church* 27-30.

To persevere in the effort to communicate Christ while at the same time respecting the freedom and pace of each soul can demand great patience of the apostle. In fact it was the *patience* of Christ in his *Passion* that brought about salvation (both words come from the Latin *patior* - "to suffer").

Some friends or acquaintances may have become disaffected from the Church for various reasons. The challenge of our apostolate then is to show the reality of the Church as a loving Mother, a theme very dear to Pope Francis. The reaction to sin and scandal should not be to leave the Church but to love her more faithfully. Perseverance in evangelisation can be constructive and fruitful reparation. Where the edifice of God's house has been damaged and disfigured by sin, we can repair it and make it more beautiful than ever by a renewed fidelity in spreading the Gospel "in season and out of season" (cf. 2 *Tm* 4:2).

Love Has the Final Word

Every effort is fruitful

No matter what the difficulties and obstacles, Christ's cross remains victorious. In virtue of the Resurrection, goodness and love have the final word. The Holy Father reminds us of the basis for this faith. He assures us repeatedly that the risen Christ is alive and active and that the mission of the Church is his mission. "Christ's resurrection is not an event of the past". For this reason, "however dark things are, goodness always emerges and spreads" (*EG* 276).

From our limited earthly vantage point we may not see the fruits of our labours. But they are always there. The mission of each of the faithful shares in the drama of the Church's journey through history such as it is described by the Second Vatican Council:

> The Church, like a stranger in a foreign land, presses forward amid the persecutions of the world and the consolations of God, announcing the cross and death of the Lord until he comes (cf. *1 Co* 11:26). But by the power of the risen Lord she is given strength to overcome, in patience and in love, her sorrows and

difficulties, both those that are from within and those that are from without, so that she may reveal in the world, faithfully, however darkly, the mystery of the Lord until, in the consummation, it shall be manifested in full light (*LG* 8).

Mary, Queen of Apostles

In his teaching Pope Francis constantly makes reference to the Blessed Virgin. He often highlights her role in spreading the Gospel. "Mary is the mother of the Church which evangelises, and without her we could never truly understand the spirit of the new evangelisation" (*EG* 284). Our Lady is the great intercessor in the apostolate, and in her person and actions, she is also a model of how to spread the joy of the Gospel.

The intervention of Our Lady at the wedding feast of Cana is an icon of evangelisation. Here we find the Mother of God among family and friends. She is attentive to their needs and goes out of her way to help them: "They have no wine" (*Jn* 2:3). Mary shows us how apostolate is always an act of love and takes place spontaneously and naturally, anywhere and everywhere, such as at this family gathering at a country wedding.

Apostolate is a beautiful task which brings great joy, as at Cana. The loving Mother's action benefitted each and all of her children. The guests rejoiced with the finest wine; the newly-married couple were spared lasting embarrassment, the steward of the feast was not shamed, the Lord's disciples grew in faith, while Christ himself "let his glory be seen" (*Jn* 2:11). Today too, we as children of Mary are confirmed and encouraged in our faith when we contemplate this first miracle of our Lord's public life.

Mary embodies the apostolic love which is the duty and privilege of all believers. This love is at once demanding and attentive, determined and tender. Our Lady shows us that evangelisation is essentially about trying to help others meet Christ.

As St Josemaría observed:

In his Gospel St John has recorded a wonderful phrase of Our Lady. At the wedding of Cana she turned to the waiters and said: "Do whatever he tells you". That's what it's all about - getting people to face Jesus and ask him: "Lord, what do you want me to do?" (*Christ is Passing By*, n. 149).

In the company of Our Lady

The Holy Father is calling all of the faithful to make their daily lives into a real proclamation of the joy of the Gospel. Pentecost is not simply an event of the past, he tells us, but is the reality of the Church here and now and until the end of time.

When the Holy Spirit descended on the first members of the Church on the day of Pentecost, they were filled with the joy of the Gospel and spread it everywhere. To prepare for the coming of the Holy Spirit, the apostles and disciples of Jesus "joined in continuous prayer, together with several women, incuding Mary the mother of Jesus" (*Ac* 1:14). The Holy Spirit urges us also to renew our zeal to spread the Gospel and we can best prepare to receive his "power from on high" (*Lk* 24:49) by being united in prayer in company with Our Lady.

We make our own the petition of Pope Francis:

Mary, Virgin and Mother,
you who, moved by the Holy Spirit,
welcomed the word of life
in the depths of your humble faith:
as you gave yourself completely to the Eternal One,
help us to say our own "yes"
to the urgent call, as pressing as ever,
to proclaim the good news of Jesus.
(...)
Obtain for us now a new ardour born of the resurrection,
that we may bring to all the Gospel of life
which triumphs over death.
Give us a holy courage to seek new paths,
that the gift of unfading beauty
may reach every man and woman (*EG* 288).